SUPER SANDCASTLE™
Super Simple Crafts

SUPER SIMPLE
Art to Wear

Fun and Easy-to-Make
Crafts for Kids

Karen Latchana Kenney

Consulting Editor, Diane Craig, M.A./Reading Specialist

ABDO
Publishing Company

Published by ABDO Publishing Company, 8000 West 78th Street, Edina, Minnesota 55439.
Copyright © 2010 by Abdo Consulting Group, Inc. International copyrights reserved in all
countries. No part of this book may be reproduced in any form without written permission from
the publisher. Super SandCastle™ is a trademark and logo of ABDO Publishing Company.

Printed in the United States.

Editor: Liz Salzmann
Content Developer: Nancy Tuminelly
Cover and Interior Design and Production: Oona Gaarder-Juntti, Mighty Media
Photo Credits: Colleen Dolphin, Shutterstock
Activity Production: Robyn Correll, Oona Gaarder-Juntti

The following manufacturers/names appearing in this book are trademarks:
Aleene's® Original Tacky Glue®, Target® Aluminum Foil, Sanford® Sharpie®, VELCRO®,
FabricMate™

Library of Congress Cataloging-in-Publication Data

Kenney, Karen Latchana.
  Super simple art to wear : fun and easy-to-make crafts for kids / Karen Latchana Kenney.
    p. cm. -- (Super simple crafts)
  ISBN 978-1-60453-622-5
  1. Handicraft--Juvenile literature. 2. Wearable art--Juvenile literature. I. Title.

TT160.K42 2010
745.5--dc22
                          2009000349

Super SandCastle™ books are created by a team of professional educators, reading
specialists, and content developers around five essential components—phonemic awareness,
phonics, vocabulary, text comprehension, and fluency—to assist young readers as they develop
reading skills and strategies and increase their general knowledge. All books are written,
reviewed, and leveled for guided reading, early reading intervention, and Accelerated Reader®
programs for use in shared, guided, and independent reading and writing activities to support a
balanced approach to literacy instruction.

To **Adult Helpers**

Making art to wear is fun and simple to do. There are just a few
things to remember to keep kids safe. Sometimes liquids, such as
rubbing alcohol or baby oil, will be used. For those activities, adult
supervision is recommended. Also, glue, paint, and markers will be
used in some activities. Make sure kids protect their clothes and
work surfaces before starting.

Table of Contents

Symbols

Look for this symbol in this book.

 Adult Help. Get help! You will
need help from an adult.

Wear Your Art!

Have you ever tried wearing your art? It's so cool! Make a new bandana or a **unique** hat. Then put it on! Show your personal style with art you can wear. It's simple! Try some or all of the **projects** in this book. It's up to you! From start to finish, making super simple art to wear is fun to do!

Tools and Supplies

Here are many of the things you will need to do the **projects** in this book. You can find them online or at your local craft store.

clear plastic tubing

thin cardboard

white shoelaces

baseball cap

cord

elastic hair bands

felt

Tacky Glue

rhinestones

beads

ribbon

nail polish

3D paint

fleece

4

rubbing alcohol

rubber bands

white bandana

bucket

aluminum foil

Velcro

cookie cutters

hole punch

permanent markers

hair clips

tape measure

glitter

plain white T-shirt

small funnel

spray bottle

fabric markers

Painted Shoelaces

Show your personal style on your shoes!

Supply List
- white shoelaces
- fabric markers
- 3D paint

1. Lay a pair of shoelaces flat on the table.

2. Color one side of each shoelace with **fabric** markers or 3D paint. Draw stripes or shapes. Write your name. Do whatever you want. Just show your style! Let the shoelaces dry.

3. Flip the shoelaces over. Color the other side of each shoelace.

4. After the shoelaces are dry, put them in your shoes.

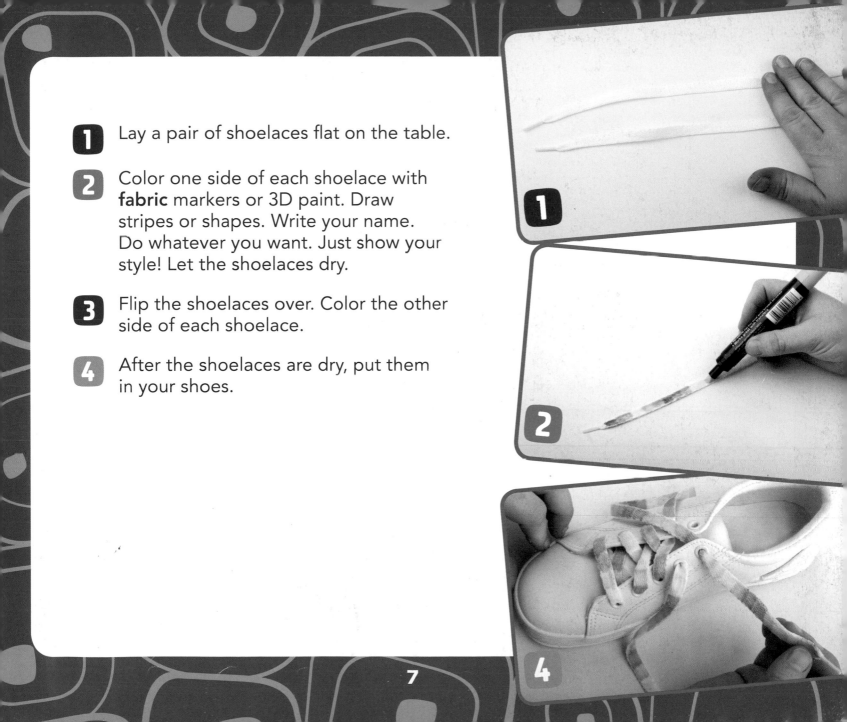

Clips and Bands

Add some sparkle and color with these pretty clips and hair bands!

Supply List

- hair clips
- colored nail polish
- rhinestones
- glitter nail polish
- elastic hair band
- colored ribbon
- ruler
- scissors
- beads (optional)

Sparkle Clips

1. Paint the top of a hair clip with colored nail polish.

2. While the polish is still wet, add a **rhinestone**. Put it at the wide end of the clip. Press it into the polish. Let it dry for a few minutes.

3. Paint the clip with a thin layer of glitter polish.

4. Let the polish dry completely before putting the clip in your hair.

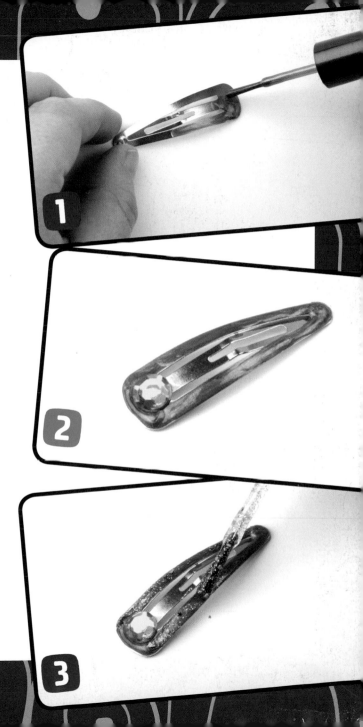

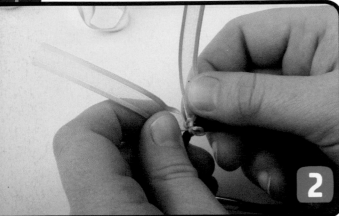

Ribbon Bands

1 Choose a hair band and two colors of **ribbon**. Cut the ribbon into pieces at least 6 inches (15 cm) long. You'll need 8 pieces of each color.

2 Tie a ribbon onto a hair band. The ends of the ribbon should be even. Make two tight knots.

3 Tie the rest of the ribbons onto the band, **alternating** colors. Try to space the ribbons evenly around the band.

More Super Ideas

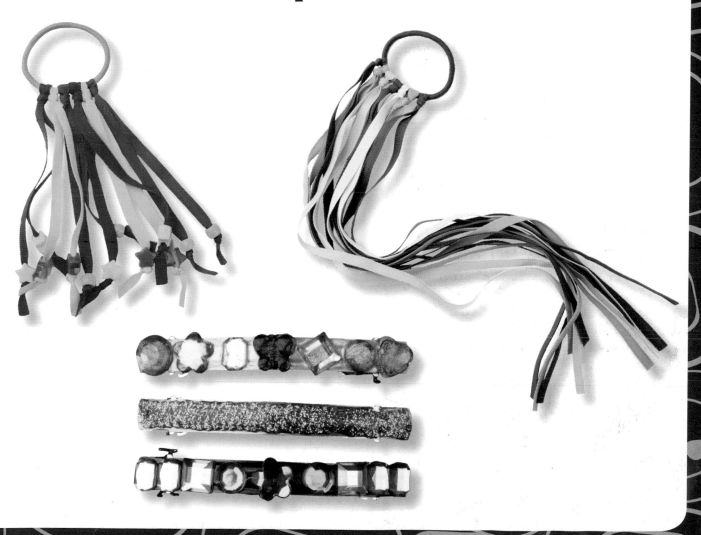

Custom Cap

Design your own hat to show your style.

1. The cap may have a **logo** on it that you want to cover up. Cut a piece of **felt** big enough to cover the logo. It can be square or round, or any shape you want. Glue the felt over the logo on the cap.

2. Think of a figure or **design** to put on your cap. Draw it on a piece of paper and cut it out. Or cut a picture you like out of a magazine.

3. Trace the figure onto felt. Cut it out and glue it on to the cap.

4. Decorate the cap. You can write your name or paint designs with 3D paint.

5. Let the glue and paint dry completely. Then wear your personalized cap with pride!

Totally You Tee

Make a T-shirt that shows how unique you are!

1. Place a cookie cutter on the cardboard. Trace around the cookie cutter with a pencil.

2. Cut out the cookie cutter shape. Make more cardboard shapes using different cookie cutters.

3. Lay the T-shirt on the table. Put another piece of cardboard inside the T-shirt.

4. Choose one of the cardboard shapes you made. Place it on the T-shirt and hold it down tightly. Trace the shape with a **fabric** marker. Remove the cardboard and color in the shape. Trace and color more shapes on the T-shirt.

5. Use the fabric markers or 3D paint to add more **designs**. Try writing your name or a fun message.

6. Let the ink and paint dry before removing the cardboard. Turn the T-shirt inside out when you wash it.

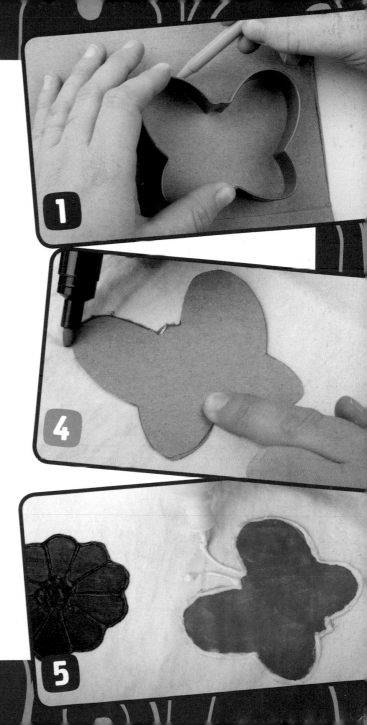

Glitter Bracelet

Turn your wrist and watch this bracelet shimmer!

16

Supply List

- ⅜ inch (9.53 mm) clear plastic tubing
- ½ inch (12.7 mm) clear plastic tubing
- scissors
- small funnel
- glitter

1. Cut a piece of the wide tube that is 1 inch (3 cm) long. Cut a piece of the narrow tube that is 8 inches (20 cm) long.

2. Push one end of the narrow tube half way through the wide tube. It should fit very tightly.

3. Ask an adult to hold the tube with a finger covering one end.

4. Stick the tip of the funnel into the other end of the tube. Add glitter a little bit at a time. Use one color or different colors. Fill the tube almost all the way.

5. Carefully bring the ends of the tube together. Stick the narrow end into the wide end. Push it as far in as you can.

Bandana-Rama

A cool way to tie-dye without making a mess!

1. Make three balls of aluminum foil. They should each be the size of your fist.

2. Lay the bandana flat on the table. Put a foil ball in the middle of the bandana.

3. Wrap the bandana tightly around the foil ball. Use two rubber bands to keep the bandana around the ball.

4. Wrap the other two foil balls in the bandana. The rubber bands should hold the bandana tightly around each ball.

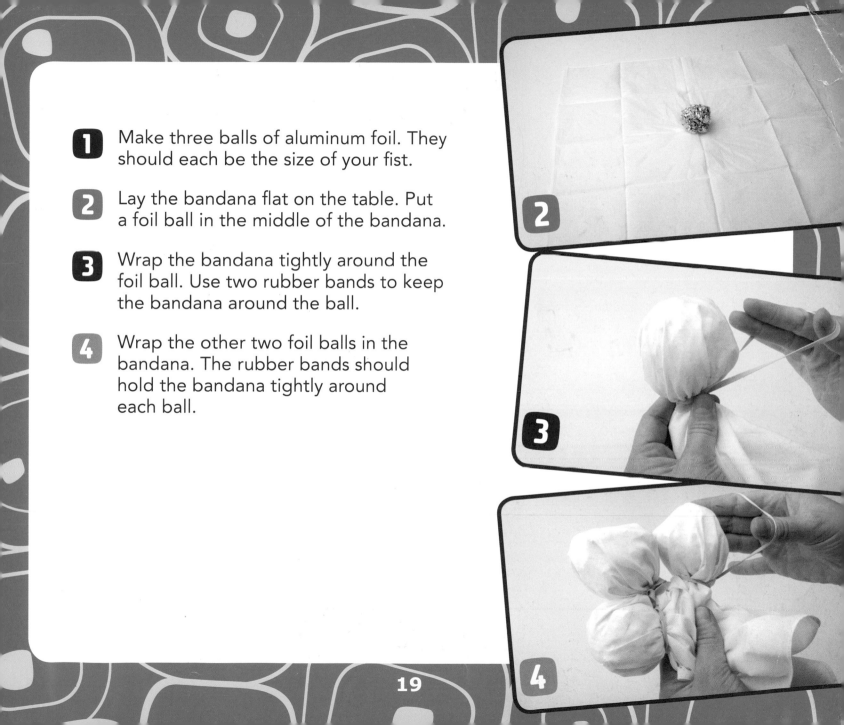

5 Color the **fabric** covering one of the balls. Use one color of **permanent** marker. Stop at the rubber band. Make sure all the fabric around the ball is colored.

6 Use a different color for the fabric around the second ball. Then use a third color for the third ball.

7 Ask an adult to help you fill the spray bottle with rubbing alcohol. Be careful not to spill!

8. Put the bandana in the bucket. Spray it all over with the rubbing alcohol. The colors will start to **bleed**. Let it dry completely.

9. Remove the rubber bands and foil balls from the bandana. Open it up and see the cool colors!

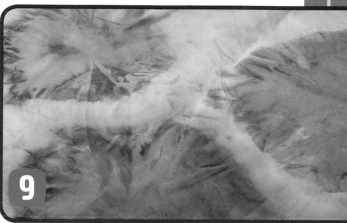

10. Ask an adult to put the bandana in the dryer on high for 30 minutes. This will help set the colors.

11. Decorate the border of your bandana! Use a **fabric** marker. Draw dots or curvy lines around the edge.

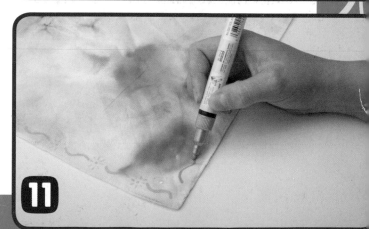

Skinny Braided Belt

Braid cord, ribbon, or yarn into a unique belt!

Supply List

- 2 colors of cord, 150 inches (381 cm) of each color
- tape measure or ruler
- scissors
- tape
- beads

1. Cut the cord into pieces that are 50 inches (127 cm) long. You should have three pieces of each color.

2. Tie all six cords together at one end. The knot should be about 8 inches (20 cm) from the end.

3. Tape the knotted end to the table. Separate the cords into three pairs. Each pair should have a cord of each color.

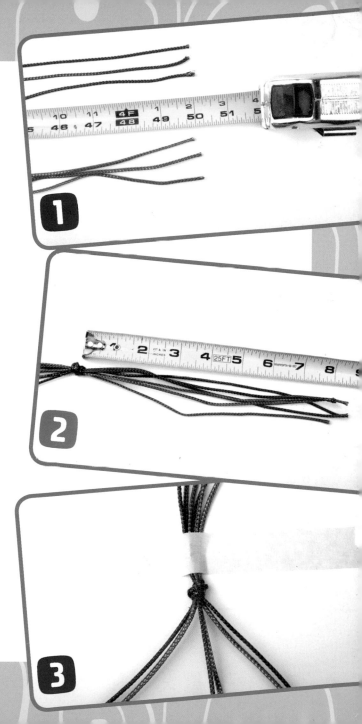

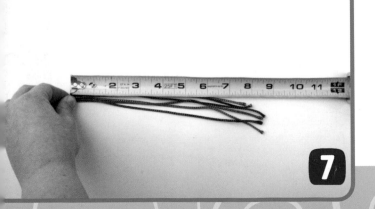

4 Start braiding the cords. Move the pair of cords on the right over the pair in the middle. The right pair becomes the middle pair.

5 Then move the pair of cords on the left over the pair in the middle. The left pair becomes the middle pair.

6 **Alternate** back and forth. Keep moving the right cords to the middle and then move the left cords to the middle. Try to keep the cords smooth as you braid them. You can pull gently to make the braid tighter.

7 Keep braiding until there are about 9 inches (23 cm) of unbraided cord left.

8 Tie a knot where the braid ends. After the knot is tied, there should be about 8 inches (20 cm) of cord left.

9 Put the end of a cord through a bead. Tie a knot in the cord to keep the bead from sliding off. You may need to tie more than one knot. Put a bead on each of the other cords.

10 To wear the belt, just tie it around your waist!

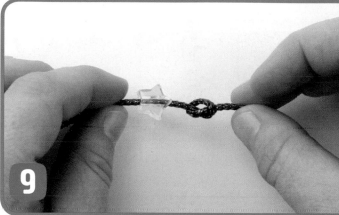

Circle Purse

Just cut and glue to make this super cute purse!

Supply List

- 2 pieces of felt that are 12 inches (30 cm) square
- permanent marker
- scissors
- ruler
- Tacky Glue
- 1-inch (3-cm) strip of Velcro
- hole punch
- ribbon
- felt scraps

1. Fold one **felt** square in half. Draw a half-circle that takes up most of the felt. The folded edge should be the straight side of the half-circle. Cut it out and unfold it so you have a circle of felt.

2. Lay the circle on the other felt square. Trace around it and cut it out. You should have two felt circles that are the same size.

3. Cut off the top 2 inches (5 cm) of one circle. The rest of that circle will be the front of the **purse**. The full circle will be the back.

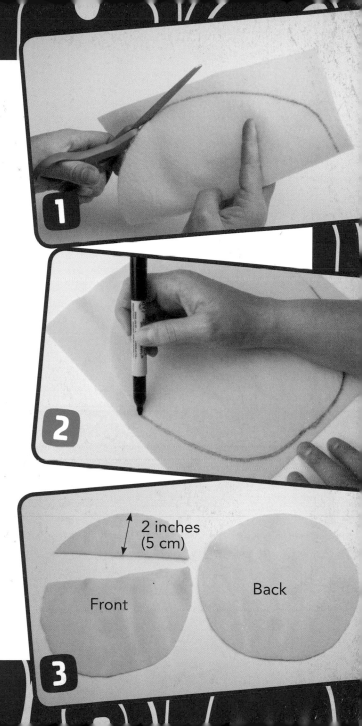

2 inches (5 cm)

Front

Back

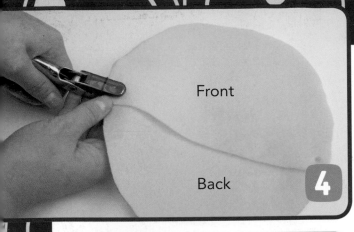

Front

Back

4

5

4 Put the front piece on top of the back piece. The curved edges of the two pieces should line up. Use a hole punch to make a hole on each side. The holes should go through both pieces. They should be near the straight edge of the front piece.

5 Put glue along the edge of the back piece. The glue should go around the bottom between the holes.

6 Lay the front piece on top of the back piece. Make sure the round edges and the holes line up. Press the pieces together.

7 Separate the strip of Velcro. Glue one side to the top of the back of the **purse**. It should be in the middle near the edge.

8 Glue the other side of the Velcro to the front of the **purse**. It should be in the middle below the straight edge.

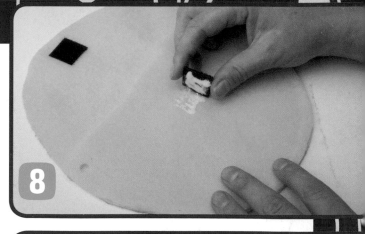

9 Cut a piece of **ribbon** 24 inches (61 cm) long. Tie one end of the ribbon to each hole.

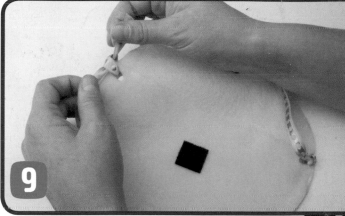

10 Fold the flap of the purse down so the Velcro holds it closed. Decorate the front of the purse. Glue a line of ribbon across the middle. Make cute circle **designs**. Glue circles on the flap and body of the purse.

11 Let the glue dry before you use your purse.

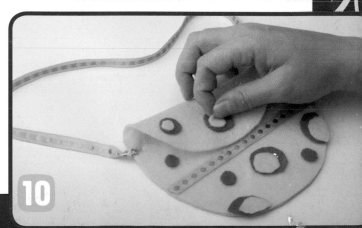

Fuzzy Fleece Scarf

Make a scarf to keep your neck warm in style!

Supply List
- fleece fabric
- scissors
- tape measure
- Tacky Glue
- felt
- 3D paint

1. Cut a piece of fleece 7 inches (18 cm) wide and 60 inches (152 cm) long.

2. Fold the fleece with the ends lined up on top of each other. Make six cuts in the ends of the fleece. Cut through both ends at the same time. The cuts should be 4 inches (10 cm) long and 1 inch (3 cm) apart.

3. Unfold the scarf and tie a knot in each strip.

4. Cut fun shapes out of **felt**. Use 3D paint to decorate the felt shapes.

5. Glue the shapes to the scarf. Completely cover the back of each shape with glue. The fleece will **absorb** some of the glue.

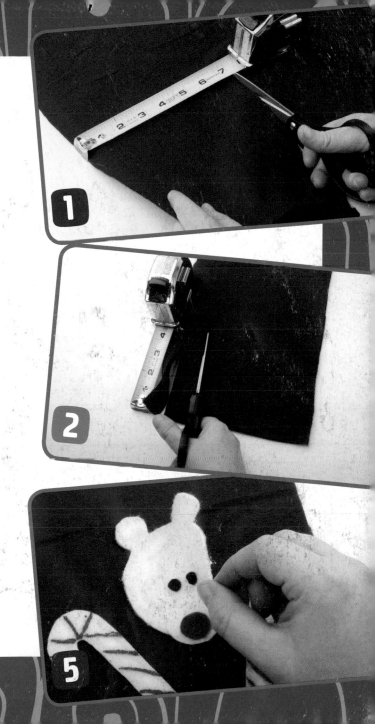

Glossary

absorb – to take in or soak up a liquid.

alternate – to change back and forth from one to the other.

bleed – to spread into neighboring areas.

design – a decorative pattern or arrangement.

fabric – woven material or cloth.

felt – a soft, thick fabric.

logo – a symbol of a company or organization.

permanent – meant to last for a very long time.

project – a task or activity.

purse – a bag for carrying money and personal items.

rhinestone – a fake jewel.

ribbon – a long, narrow strip of material.

unique – the only one of its kind.

About SUPER SANDCASTLE™

Bigger Books for Emerging Readers
Grades K–4

Created for library, classroom, and at-home use, Super SandCastle™ books support and engage young readers as they develop and build literacy skills and will increase their general knowledge about the world around them. Super SandCastle™ books are an extension of SandCastle™, the leading preK–3 imprint for emerging and beginning readers. Super SandCastle™ features a larger trim size for more reading fun.

Let Us Know

Super SandCastle™ would like to hear your stories about reading this book. What was your favorite page? Was there something hard that you needed help with? Share the ups and downs of learning to read. We want to hear from you! Send us an e-mail.

sandcastle@abdopublishing.com

Contact us for a complete list of SandCastle™, Super SandCastle™, and other nonfiction and fiction titles from ABDO Publishing Company.

www.abdopublishing.com • 8000 West 78th Street Edina, MN 55439 • 800-800-1312 • 952-831-1632 fax